Kevin Volans

ASANGA

for Solo Percussion

1997

CH 61488

CHESTER MUSIC

EXCLUSIVELY DISTRIBUTED BY

Asanga was written for Robyn Schulkowsky who gave a preview performance on 12 June 1998 at the Deutsches Theater, Berlin. She gave the world première on 30 September 1998 in Fylkingen, Stockholm.

Asanga is a Sanskrit word meaning 'freedom from attachment'.

Instrumentation

Four low drums (including bass drum) and two higher tom-toms, plus two high metal plates or extremely high skins.

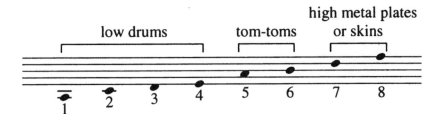

The drums should be played with mallets or sticks that give an articulate and centred sound.

Duration: c. 8 minutes

for Robyn Schulkowsky

ASANGA
for Solo Percussion

Kevin Volans
(1997)

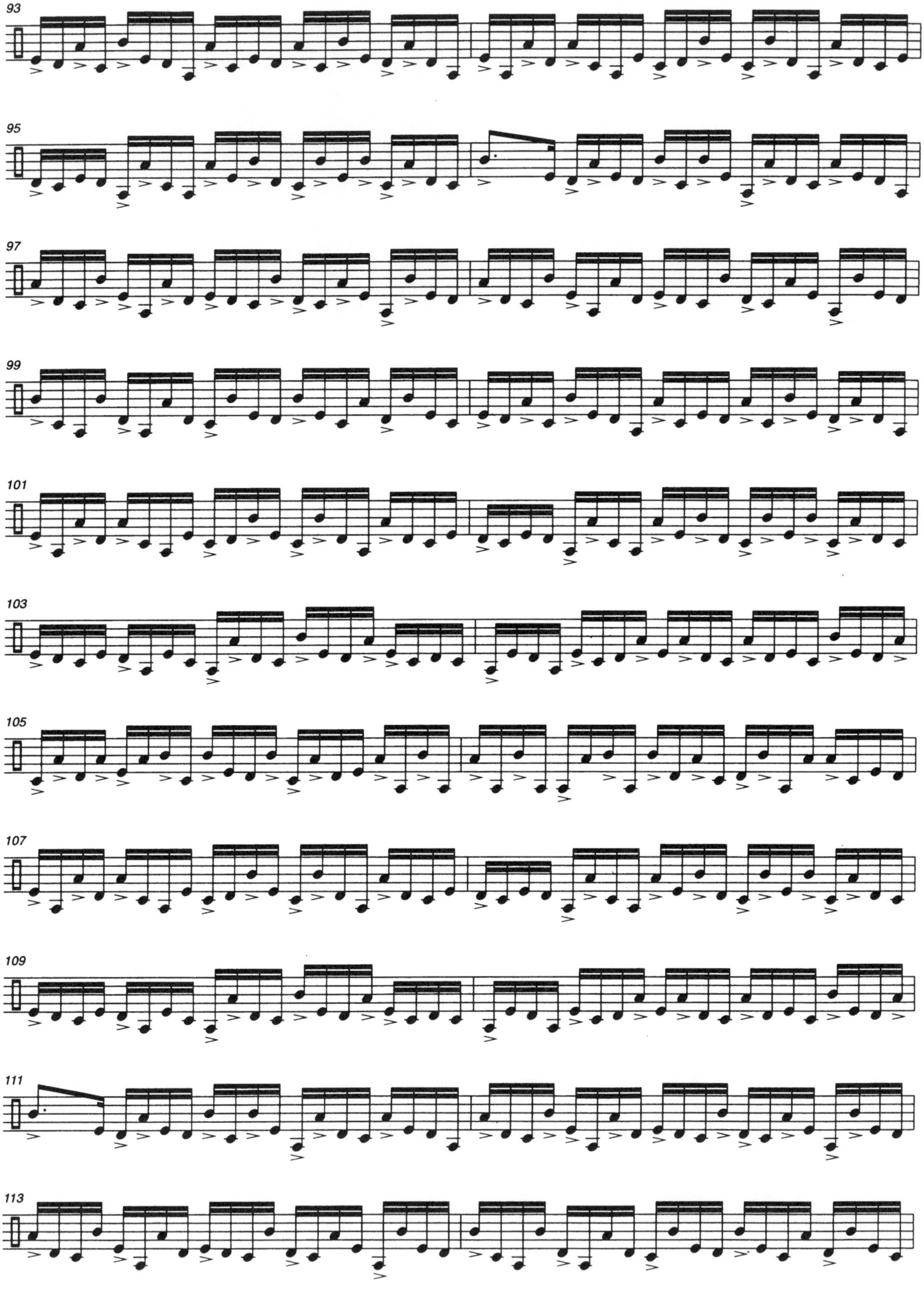
93
95
97
99
101
103
105
107
109
111
113

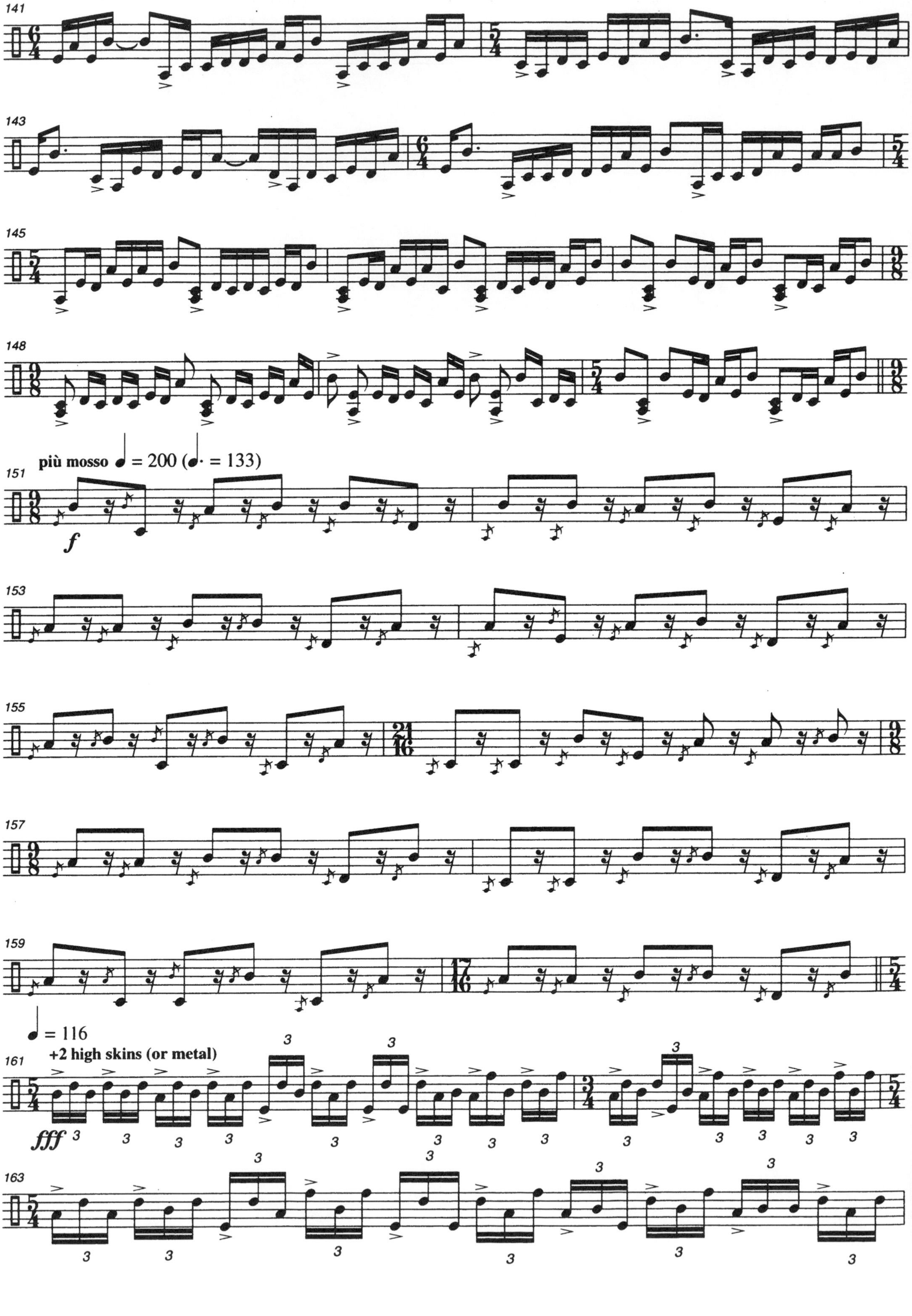
più mosso ♩ = 200 (♩. = 133)
♩ = 116
+2 high skins (or metal)
fff